A Guide for Using

Crispin:
The Cross of Lead

in the Classroom

Based on the book written by Avi

*This guide written by **Melissa Hart, M.F.A.***

Teacher Created Materials, Inc.
6421 Industry Way
Westminster, CA 92683
www.teachercreated.com
©2004 Teacher Created Materials
Made in U.S.A.
ISBN 0-7439-3162-9

Editor
Janet Cain, M.Ed.

Illustrator
Alexandra Artigas

Cover Artist
Kevin Barnes

Table of Contents

Introduction

A good book can enrich our lives like a good friend. Fictional characters can inspire us and teach us about the world in which we live. We can turn to books for companionship, entertainment, and guidance. A truly beloved book may touch our lives forever.

In *Literature Units*, great care has been taken to select books that are sure to become your students' good friends!

Teachers who use this unit will find the following features to supplement their own ideas:

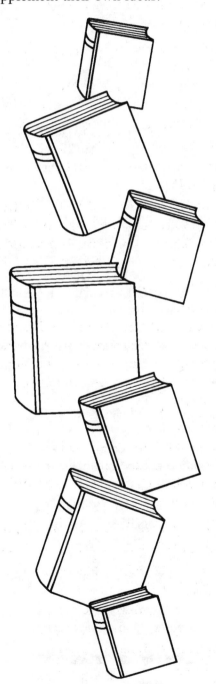

- Sample Lesson Plans
- Pre-Reading Activities
- A Biographical Sketch and Picture of the Author
- A Book Summary
- Vocabulary Lists and Suggested Vocabulary Activities
- Chapters grouped for study, with each section including:
  - *quizzes*
  - *hands-on projects*
  - *cooperative learning activities*
  - *cross-curricular connections*
  - *extensions into the reader's life*
- Post-Reading Activities
- Book Report Ideas
- Research Activities
- Culminating Activities
- Three Different Options for Unit Tests
- Bibliography
- Answer Key

We are certain this unit will be a valuable addition to your own curriculum ideas for *Crispin: The Cross of Lead.*

Sample Lesson Plans

Each of the lessons suggested below can take from one to several days to complete.

LESSON 1

- Introduce and complete some or all of the pre-reading activities from "Before the Book." (page 5)
- Read "About the Author" with students. (page 6)
- Introduce the vocabulary list for Section 1. (page 8)

LESSON 2

- Read Chapters 1–12. As you read, place the vocabulary words in the context of the story and discuss their meanings.
- Locate England and France on a world map.
- Choose a vocabulary activity to complete. (page 9)
- Make a leather pouch. (page 11)
- Design a village. (page 12)
- Learn about kings, stewards, and peasants. (page 13)
- Reflect on being cast out. (page 14)
- Administer the Section 1 Quiz. (page 10)
- Introduce the vocabulary list for Section 2. (page 8)

LESSON 3

- Read Chapters 13–24. As you read, place the vocabulary words in the context of the story and discuss their meanings.
- Choose a vocabulary activity to complete. (page 9)
- Learn to juggle. (page 16)
- Learn about priests. (page 17)
- Investigate the Plague. (page 18)
- Ask yourself questions. (page 19)
- Administer the Section 2 quiz. (page 15)
- Introduce the vocabulary list for Section 3. (page 8)

LESSON 4

- Read Chapters 25–35. As you read, place the vocabulary words in the context of the story and discuss their meanings.
- Choose a vocabulary activity to complete. (page 9)
- Play the recorder. (page 21)
- Track observations. (page 22)
- Research Renaissance personalities. (page 23)
- Think about being different. (page 24)
- Administer the Section 3 Quiz. (page 20)
- Introduce the vocabulary list for Section 4. (page 8)

LESSON 5

- Read Chapters 36–47. As you read, place the vocabulary words in the context of the story and discuss their meanings.
- Choose a vocabulary activity to complete. (page 9)
- Bake bread. (page 26)
- Research class struggles. (page 27)
- Write using sensory details. (page 28)
- Describe your marketplace. (page 29)
- Administer the Section 4 Quiz. (page 25)
- Introduce the vocabulary list for section 5. (page 8)

LESSON 6

- Read Chapters 48–58. As you read, place the vocabulary words in the context of the story and discuss their meanings.
- Choose a vocabulary activity to complete. (page 9)
- Make candles. (page 31)
- Give the gift of reading. (page 32)
- Learn about the Renaissance world. (page 33)
- Think about courage. (page 34)
- Administer the Section 5 Quiz. (page 30)

LESSON 7

- Discuss questions students have about the book. (page 35)
- Assign a book report and research activity. (pages 36–37)
- Begin work on one or more culminating activities. (pages 38–42)

LESSON 8

- Choose and administer one or more of the Unit Tests. (pages 43–45)
- Discuss students' feelings about the book.
- Provide a bibliography of related reading. (page 46)

     4

Before the Book

Before you begin reading *Crispin: The Cross of Lead* with your students, complete one or more of the following pre-reading activities to stimulate their interest and enhance comprehension.

1. Examine the cover of the book. Ask students to predict the book's plot, characters, and setting.

2. Discuss the title. See if students can predict anything about the story from its title.

3. Pose the following questions and ask the students to respond:

> - Why would an entire village be unkind to a poverty-stricken child with no father?
>
> - How is religion important in some people's lives?
>
> - Why might someone have to escape from the town where he/she grew up?
>
> - Why might an older person want to help a child?
>
> - What can you learn simply by using your powers of observation?
>
> - How would you feel if you learned something important about your parents that you never knew?
>
> - Have you ever done something brave even though you were scared?
>
> - What is self-confidence? How does a person become self-confident?
>
> - What does *freedom* mean? Why is it important to have freedom?
>
> - Why is a person's name important? What would it be like to have no name?

4. Direct students to work in groups to brainstorm how a child might cope with losing both parents. Ask them to share their ideas with the class.

5. Ask students to work in groups to list the different reasons religion is important to certain people. Discuss different religions and how they help people.

6. Direct students to work in groups to brainstorm what a child might do if he/she had to leave a childhood home and travel alone. How would a child find food and shelter? Where would the child go?

7. Have students work in groups to make a list of courageous acts people might undertake despite their fears. Begin the assignment with a reflection about firefighters, police officers, and surgeons, but remind students that even doing something ordinary, such as agreeing to go to the dentist when one is scared, can be considered courageous.

About the Author

Avi Wortis was born in New York City on December 23, 1937. His parents were involved with civil rights and other social justice issues, which created a lively household. His father worked as a doctor, and his mother was a social worker. When he was a year old, his twin sister Emily gave him the name "Avi," and now he uses no other.

As a child, Avi did not care for sports, but he loved playing games that relied on his imagination. He read comic books, built models, went to the movies, and listened to children's radio. Every night, his parents read to him, and, every Friday, they took him to the library. Avi did well in science, but in high school, he failed all of his courses. He suffers from *dysgraphia* — a writing impairment that causes him to reverse letters and misspell words. After he flunked out of public high school, his parents put him in a small, private school that focused on reading and writing.

Although his family discouraged him from becoming a writer, Avi began to write plays when he was seventeen. "I think you become a writer when you stop writing for yourself or your teachers and start thinking about readers," he says. He believes reading is the key to writing; the more you read, the better you'll write. Some of Avi's favorite authors are Robert Louis Stevenson, Ernest Hemingway, and Charles Dickens.

Avi worked as a children's librarian for 25 years before he began to write professionally. It was only after Avi had sons of his own that he began to write for children. His first book was published in 1970. He has had over 45 books published since then. Each book takes Avi about a year and a half to write. He writes a draft, then rewrites the manuscript several times. Every day, he gets up at five or six in the morning to write. He prefers to work on a computer in a quiet space. He loves the rewriting process because he gets to make the story better and better.

Avi writes mystery, adventure, fantasy, and ghost stories. Three of his books, *The True Confession of Charlotte Doyle, Nothing But the Truth,* and *Crispin: The Cross of Lead,* were named Newbery Honor Award Books — the most prestigious award in children's literature. He has also won the *Boston Globe-Horn Book Award* for Fiction. Avi enjoys writing historical fiction, like *Crispin,* because it allows him to use a story to illustrate the injustices of past eras. *Crispin* follows the struggles of the working class, allowing the author to comment on how he believes our contemporary society can improve. "We who write historical fiction get to alter the future," he says. He gets ideas for books by observing people, things, and situations. Following *Crispin,* Avi wrote *The Mayor of Central Park,* about a romantic squirrel living in New York City. His greatest hope is that his books are fun to read, as well as memorable.

In addition to writing, Avi loves to visit schools and meet his readers. He always asks to speak to the students with learning disabilities. He brings them pages of his manuscripts and points out the misspelled words and grammatical mistakes, which gives them hope for their own writing.

Crispin: The Cross of Lead

By Avi

(Hyperion Books for Children, 2002)

Thirteen-year old Crispin buries his mother, with the help of the village priest. That night, he witnesses the steward of the manor, John Aycliffe, in a secret meeting with another man. John Aycliffe discovers Crispin, but the boy escapes. The steward declares Crispin "a wolf's head," and orders him killed. The village priest gives Crispin a cross of lead that belonged to his mother and shocks the boy by revealing that his mother could both read and write.

Crispin flees his village of Stromford, pursued by the steward and his men. Crispin wanders alone until he comes upon a village devastated by the Plague. It is here that he meets a juggler named Bear. Bear demands that Crispin become his servant, and reluctantly, the boy swears his servitude. Bear teaches Crispin how to juggle and play the recorder, so they can earn money by performing as they travel. But, as Bear and Crispin approach a small village, they spot John Aycliffe and his men waiting on the road for Crispin. They quickly alter their travel plans.

Bear and Crispin enter the village of Lodgecot, where they entertain the locals and learn that the entire countryside is on the lookout for Crispin. They leave the village, but not before they attract the attention of a one-eyed man who regards them with suspicion. Bear and Crispin approach the gates of Great Wexly, and, in a clever maneuver, get through the gates without being seen.

Crispin is astounded at the size of the town. However, Bear asks him to remain in the room of a lodging house maintained by the Widow Daventry while he has an important meeting. Restless, Crispin disobeys Bear and escapes to see the town for himself. But he is discovered by John Aycliffe in a cathedral and flees back to Bear. Gradually, Crispin becomes aware that Bear is a spy involved in a rebellion against the British ruling class. He sees a man following Bear on the way to a meeting and rushes out of the lodging house to tell him. When he finally locates Bear with a group of rebels, he is dismayed to find soldiers on the verge of discovering them. He alerts the rebels, and all escape except for Bear.

The Widow Daventry reveals shocking news to Crispin about his parents and the lead cross. In spite of the danger to himself, Crispin resolves to win Bear's freedom. He finds a way into the palace, where he is again discovered by John Aycliffe. Aycliffe promises to let Bear go if Crispin gives him his lead cross. However, at the town gates, the steward goes back on his promise and tries to kill Bear. Bear and Crispin fight to win their freedom, learning for themselves that "in the midst of death there's life."

Vocabulary Lists

Below are lists of vocabulary words for each section of chapters. A variety of ideas for using this vocabulary in classroom activities are offered on page 9.

Section 1 (Chapters 1–12)

shroud	pinnacle
transgression	canonical
poaching	treason
cloying	tonsured
kin	scrutinized
transfixed	midwifery
curfew	foreboding
mercenary	tumult

Section 2 (Chapters 13–24)

grotesquely	tyranny
pillaged	default
sustenance	surname
trepidation	lamenting
raucously	servile
evasively	punctilious
cur	mummers
corrupt	bravado

Section 3 (Chapters 25–35)

reverence	gambols	portentous
leagues	malevolence	heirs
meandered	enraptured	illegitimate
spinney	rueful	succeed
solemnity	humors	
mollify	gauntlet	

Section 4 (Chapters 36–47)

tumultuous	vestibule	guild
buffeting	celestial	trenchers
palfrey	serpentine	caterwauling
sumptuous	laggards	disconsolate
beguiled	fervor	
abacus	wend	

Section 5 (Chapters 48–58)

agitated	scabrous	vexed
wedlock	omen	impaled
quickened	cowls	brandished
infatuated	succumb	unfettered
claimant	voracious	
bondage	parched	

8

Vocabulary Activity Ideas

You can help your students learn the vocabulary words in *Crispin: The Cross of Lead* by providing them with the stimulating vocabulary activities below.

1. Ask your students to work in groups to create an **Illustrated Book** of the vocabulary words and their meanings.

2. Separate students into groups. Use the vocabulary words to create **Crossword Puzzles** and **Word Searches**. Groups can trade puzzles with each other and complete them.

3. Play **Guess the Definition**. One student writes down the correct definition of the vocabulary word. The others write down false definitions, close enough to the original definition that their classmates might be fooled. Read all definitions, and then challenge students to guess the correct one. The students whose definitions mislead their classmates get a point for each student fooled.

4. Write a **Short Story** using as many of the words as possible. Students may then read their stories in groups.

5. Encourage your students to use each new vocabulary word in a **Conversation** five times during one day. They can take notes on how and when the word was used, and then share their experience with the class.

6. Play **Vocabulary Charades**. Each student or group of students gets a word to act out. Other students must guess the word.

7. Play **Vocabulary Pictures**. Each student or group of students must draw a picture representing a word on the chalkboard or on paper. Other students must guess the word.

8. Challenge students to a **Vocabulary Bee**. In groups or separately, students must spell the word correctly, and give its proper definition.

9. Talk about **Parts of Speech** by discussing the different forms that a word may take. For instance, some words may function as nouns, as well as verbs. The word "shroud" is a good example of a word which can be both a noun and a verb. Some words that look alike may have completely different meanings. For example, in *Crispin*, "shroud" refers to a burial garment, but it can also function as a verb that means "to cover for protection."

10. Ask your students to make **Flash Cards** with the word printed on one side and the definition printed on the other. Ask your students to work with a younger class to help them learn the definitions of the new words, using the flash cards.

11. Create **Word Art** by writing the words with glue on stiff paper and then covering the glue with glitter or sand. Alternatively, students may write the words with a squeeze bottle full of jam on bread to create an edible lesson!

Add your own ideas to this list. Attempt to have students experience vocabulary on a personal level to increase their vocabulary acquisition.

Quiz Time!

Answer the following questions about Chapters 1–12.

1. What happened to Crispin's father, according to Asta? _____

   _____

   _____

2. What does Crispin witness John Aycliffe doing in the forest one night? _____

   _____

   _____

3. What happens to the house in which Crispin grew up? _____

   _____

   _____

4. Why is Crispin labeled "a wolf's head"? _____

   _____

   _____

5. Do the people in Crispin's village believe he stole from the manor? Explain your answer.

   _____

   _____

6. What surprising things does the priest tell Crispin about his mother? _____

   _____

   _____

7. What items does Goodwife Peregrine give Crispin?_____

   _____

   _____

8. What happens when Crispin takes Cedric's advice about which direction to travel?

   _____

   _____

Make a Leather Pouch

Before Crispin leaves his childhood home of Stromford, the Widow Peregrine gives him food and offers him something for protection. Crispin describes what happened, "I stepped forward reluctantly. She reached up and dropped a thong — with a small leather pouch — about my neck. Then she spoke some words I didn't understand."

In this activity, you will make a leather pouch like the one that held Crispin's cross and three seeds.

Materials

- 2.5" x 9" (7 cm x 23 cm) pieces of genuine or imitation leather fabric
- 3' (91 cm) leather lacing
- 6 colored wooden beads
- rubber mallet

- wooden block
- glue
- nail (Make sure the diameter of the nail is a little larger than the diameter of the lacing.)

Directions

1. To make a "needle," cut one end of your piece of leather lacing at an angle, and put a few drops of glue on it. Let the glue dry.

2. Fold up 3" (7.5 cm) of the leather fabric to form a pouch. Place the pouch on a wooden block. Using the mallet and the nail, punch holes through both layers of the leather that are spaced at about every ½" (1 cm). Try to make the holes evenly spaced. Repeat on the other side.

3. Tie a knot at the end of the leather lacing that is opposite the "needle." String three beads on the leather lacing and push them down to rest against the knot. Start at one bottom corner and poke the lacing through the first hole from the back. Go through both layers of leather. Continue weaving the leather lacing in and out of holes until one side is sewn up. The lacing should not be too tight, or the leather will bunch up. However, if it is too loose, your treasures will fall out.

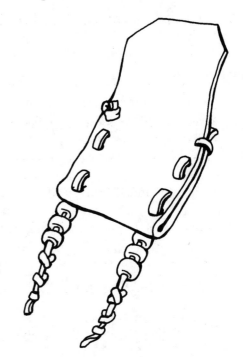

4. After you are finished lacing up one side, loop the leather lacing around your neck to determine how low you want your pouch to hang. Then begin sewing with the lacing on the other side, starting with the top corner and working your way down to the bottom corner.

5. Finish your pouch by stringing three more beads after your final hole. Then tie another knot to secure the lacing. Cut off any extra lacing.

6. Now that your pouch is finished, what will you put in it?

Design a Village

Crispin returns to the forest after the bailiff and the reeve demolish his cottage. He observes his village while standing on a high rock. He sees the blue sky, the green trees, and the river Strom, as well as the crosses that mark the village boundaries. Then he notices Lord Furnival's manor, the mill with its grinding wheels, the stone church, and forty cottages and huts. North of the village, Crispin sees the commons, the archery butts, and land for growing crops. He also sees the public stocks and gallows.

Materials for Each Group

- 3' x 3' x ¼" (91 cm x 91 cm x 0.6 cm) piece of plywood

- small square, rectangular, and cylindrical cardboard containers

- 8" x 11" (20 cm x 28 cm) sheets of thin cardboard or poster board

- pencil

- colored construction paper

- markers

- scissors

- glue

- straw

- sand

- fake grass

- tissue paper

- glitter

Directions

1. Work with three or four students to design the village of Stromford, using details from Chapter 4 of *Crispin: The Cross of Lead*. First, determine the layout of Crispin's village. Use the piece of plywood as your base. With a pencil, mark the placement of the manor, mill, church, and cottages. Note the location of other important areas as described in the novel.

2. Create the manor, mill, church, and cottages using the cardboard containers. Pay particular attention to the description of each in Chapter 4. Cover the boxes by gluing colored construction paper on to them. Use markers to decorate the buildings. Do not forget to include details, such as the bell at the church and the grinding wheel at the mill.

3. Place the buildings you have created on the plywood.

4. Use pieces of cardboard or poster board to design features, such as the archery butts, livestock, crosses, and gallows. Place these according to their location as described in the novel.

5. Indicate the commons, fields, and rivers using sand, straw, fake grass, tissue paper, and glitter.

Kings, Stewards, Peasants

Crispin's entire world is ruled by kings, lords, and the wicked steward, John Aycliffe. In medieval times, peasants were slaves who had to work from dawn until dusk with little to eat and no hope of a better future. Use a biographical dictionary, an encyclopedia, and/or the Internet to research how life differed during the fourteenth century, according to one's rank. Define each rank, below, and then write a brief description of how someone of this rank might live.

Rank	Definition of Rank	Lifestyle
King		
Lord		
Steward		
Jester		
Peasant		

Cast Out

Other than the priest, Crispin's mother had no friends. The other villagers would often make fun of her, and they looked down upon her son. After Asta dies, Crispin is forced to leave the village in which he grew up. John Aycliffe declares him "a wolf's head" and says that anyone may kill him. Feeling confused and full of sorrow, Crispin flees Stromford.

Think of a time in your life that you felt cast out or different from other people. It might be a time that you voted differently than the majority of the class, or you liked a certain item of clothing or a song that no one else liked, or you could not do something that everyone else was doing because you were ill, or you believed something that no one else believed.

Answer the following questions about a time you felt cast out or different.

1. How old were you at the time of the incident?

   _____

2. Where were you at this time?

   _____

3. What happened that made you feel cast out or different? Describe the incident using specific details. _____

4. Who was involved in making you feel cast out or different?

   _____

5. How did you express your feelings during this incident?

   _____

6. What or who caused the situation to get better?

   _____

7. What did you learn from this experience?

   _____

8. What advice would you give to someone who is feeling cast out or different from others?

   _____

   _____

   _____

   _____

   _____

Quiz Time!

Answer the following questions about Chapters 13–24.

1. What items does Crispin find in the leather pouch, and what does he do with them?

_____

_____

2. What does Crispin see that makes him want to stay alive?

_____

_____

3. How do you think Bear feels about England's government?

_____

_____

4. Why does Crispin have to serve Bear?

_____

_____

5. Why might it be important to know how to read in Crispin's era?

_____

_____

6. What does Crispin learn about Lord Furnivel from Bear?

_____

_____

7. Why does Bear advise Crispin to lose his sorrows?

_____

_____

8. If Crispin were to live by questions, what would they be?

_____

_____

Learn to Juggle

Bear does many things that surprise Crispin, not the least of which is juggling. Crispin states, "At length, however, he reached over and took up his sack and rummaged through it. From it he took out three balls, each made of stitched leather. To my surprise he tossed the balls into the air. Instead of falling to the ground, they stayed in the air and rotated at his will, with only the smallest touch and encouragement of his fingers."

Use the following activity to learn how to juggle. You will need three balls, each about the size and weight of a small apple.

Directions

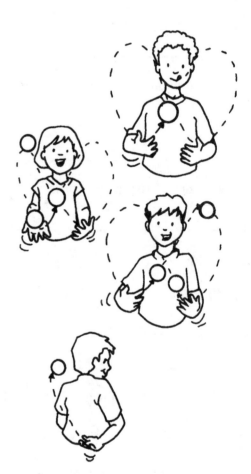

1. Imagine two focus spots (one to the right and one to the left) about a foot in front of your forehead. Hold your arms at waist level with your hands out naturally in front of you. Start with a ball in your right hand, while your left hand is empty. Toss the ball across to the focus spot on your left, and catch the ball in your left hand. Now, use your left hand to toss the ball to the focus spot on your right and catch it in your right hand. Each time, be sure to toss the ball easily and gently toward the focus spot. Do not put a spin on the ball. Practice until you can do this without dropping the ball.

2. Now hold two balls in your right hand: one at the base of your fingers and one at the back of your palm. Hold the third ball in your left hand. Toss the first ball, which is at the base of your fingers, toward your left hand. When the first ball starts on its way down, toss the second ball from your left hand and catch the first ball in your left hand as it comes down. Catch the second ball in your right hand. Practice until you can do this easily, remembering to concentrate on your focus spots.

3. Now repeat the second step, as described above. But this time, as the second ball is on its way down, toss the third ball from your right hand and catch it in your left. Toss the balls from the inside of your hands, and catch them on the outside. To keep your timing consistent, say "left" and "right" as you throw from each hand. Practice until you can consistently catch the balls.

4. Repeat the above step, adding one more toss each time you get comfortable with a series of exchanges. You can now practice juggling balls higher, lower, standing on one foot, and with your eyes closed. You can even juggle apples and oranges!

Crispin: The Cross of Lead

What About Priests?

Father Quinel is the only person in Stromford who shows kindness to Crispin. Later, Bear tells Crispin, "If you can read, you're treated as a priest. Common law does not allow priests to be hanged."

Priests and monks played a very different role from kings, lords, stewards, and peasants in the medieval world. They were less concerned with ruling or serving and more concerned with living a holy life.

Work with three or four other students to research the lives of priests during the fourteenth century, using nonfiction books, reference books, and/or the Internet. Record your findings below.

1. Describe where priests lived. _____

   _____

2. Describe where priests slept. _____

   _____

3. Explain how priests earned money for food. _____

   _____

4. Describe what a priest might have eaten on a daily basis. _____

   _____

5. Explain how priests dressed, and why they wore these particular clothes. _____

   _____

6. Describe the jobs priests did. _____

   _____

7. Explain how people treated priests. _____

   _____

8. What advantages and disadvantages were there to being a priest? _____

   _____

   _____

The Plague

The plague, also called the Great Mortality or the Pestilence, decimated Europe. Writers of the time estimated that this illness killed 20–40% of Europeans. The plague started in Asia in the early 1340s and spread to Europe in 1347. Most people who caught the plague fell gravely ill, and they were dead within a week. Research details on the plague of the fourteenth century using books, encyclopedias, and/or the Internet. Answer the questions below.

1. How did the plague spread from person to person?

_____

_____

_____

2. Describe at least three symptoms of the plague?

_____

_____

_____

3. How did people attempt to keep the plague from spreading?

_____

_____

_____

4. How did doctors attempt to treat people ill with the plague? What remedies did they use?

_____

_____

_____

5. How many people died during the plague of the 14th century?

_____

_____

_____

6. Bonus Question: How were English theaters affected during the plague?

_____

_____

_____

Now, on a separate sheet of paper, pretend you are a person living at the time of the plague. Describe what you see, hear, and feel. Use specific details to give your description authenticity.

Living by Questions

Bear tells Crispin that questions keep you living. At the end of Chapter 24, Crispin asks himself what it would be like to live by questions and what questions they would be. Crispin says, "About my father? And those things Father Quinel had said about my mother — if they be true or not. And maybe — I allowed — I'd ask what was to be *my* fate."

If you were to live your life by questions, what might those questions be? Think about the mysteries in your life. Are you confused about your family history? Do you want to know where you will get your education and what you will study? Do you wonder what your career will be? Are you curious about where you might live in the future? Write eight questions you might live by, and then write possible answers below them.

1. _____

_____

2. _____

_____

3. _____

_____

4. _____

_____

5. _____

_____

6. _____

_____

7. _____

_____

8. _____

_____

Quiz Time!

Answer the following questions about Chapters 25–35.

1. Why does Bear cut Crispin's hair and ask him to wash his face, then look at his reflection?

   _____

   _____

2. What does Crispin realize about Bear's threats and warnings to him?

   _____

   _____

3. Why does Bear teach Crispin how to play the recorder?

   _____

   _____

4. How does the village of Lodgecot remind Crispin of his own village of Stromford?

   _____

   _____

5. What does Crispin observe about the one-eyed man in Lodgecot?

   _____

   _____

6. What does Bear teach Crispin about eye contact?

   _____

   _____

7. How does the relationship between Bear and Crispin change in this section of the book?

   _____

   _____

8. How do Crispin and Bear get through the gates of Great Wexly?

   _____

   _____

Playing the Recorder

Bear teaches Crispin to play music on the recorder. Crispin recalls, "He began by instructing me about the pipe's holes — the stops, he called them — and the way to shape my mouth around the blowing end, how to shift my fingers, how to make different sounds. Reluctantly, I took up the recorder, and with fingers like soft clay, tried to play. What came out were sorry, shallow squeaks."

Here are instructions for playing a simple tune on the recorder! (Make sure each student has a recorder for this activity).

Directions

1. Using your right hand, hold your recorder in front of you. Make sure that the back of the recorder (the side with only one hole) is facing you. Using your left hand, place the fleshy part of your thumb over the bottom thumb hole. Now place your left pointer finger over the top hole on the front of the recorder, making sure that you cover the hole with the fingerprint part of your finger, not the tip of your finger. Continue to hold the recorder with your left hand. With the palm of your right hand facing away from you, count down four holes from the top, and place your right thumb behind the fourth hole.

2. Practice these three notes: B, A, and G. Look at the chart and the pictures to help you.

3. Now you will learn to play a song called "Hot Cross Buns." The song is named after hot cross buns, which are made of sweet bread dough that is full of raisins and currents. The buns are traditionally served on Good Friday. Before baking the buns, the cook slashes an "X" across the top. When the buns are cool, the cook fills the X with icing.

Tracking Observations

In Chapter 27 of *Crispin: The Cross of Lead*, Bear suddenly halts when he sees a flock of wood pigeons swirling overhead. He follows the pigeons and discovers John Aycliffe and his men waiting below the summit to kill Crispin. Crispin states, "As we went along, I kept thinking how Bear had noticed the birds, which allowed him to see the soldiers. If, I told myself, I was to stay alive in this new world, I must learn such skills as he had."

People have long studied animals, birds, and plants to learn more about their environment. Work with two or three other students to research and record how the creatures and plants on the list below might help humans learn about their environment. Use the Internet, reference books, and/or nonfiction books to locate information. The first one has been done for you.

Animal/Plant	What It Might Teach Us
1. Your dog barks.	There is someone at the front door.
2. A rooster crows.	
3. A groundhog comes out of its den on a winter day.	
4. A daffodil blooms.	
5. The leaves on a tree turn red and yellow.	
6. A cat's coat grows thicker.	
7. Blackberries ripen.	
8. A rabbit runs to get under a bush.	
9. Geese are flying south.	
10. Deciduous trees have lost all their leaves.	

Renaissance Personalities

The era in which Crispin lived was full of interesting people who did amazing things. Use the Internet, nonfiction books, and/or reference books to answer the following questions about famous people from the Renaissance. The first one has been done for you.

Who Am I?	What Did I Do?
1. Donatello	I was a great Italian sculptor. I sculpted out of bronze.
2. Marco Polo	
3. Michelangelo Buonarroti	
4. Christopher Columbus	
5. Galileo Galilei	
6. Catherine De Medici	
7. William Shakespeare	
8. Rene Descartes	
9. Isabella d'Este	
10. Elizabeth I	

Different Than You Are

Crispin believes he cannot improve himself. Bear argues with him, finally cutting his hair and making him wash his face. "Have you ever desired to be anything different from what you are?" Bear asks the boy.

Think about who you are. What traits do you appreciate about yourself? What aspects of yourself would you like to change? How would you go about changing the things you don't like about yourself? Write your answers below.

List ten things you like about yourself.

1.
2.
3.
4.
5.
6.
7.
8.
9.
10.

List five things about yourself that you might like to change. After each, list one way you might go about making that change. Study the example below.

What I Would Like to Change	How I Might Make That Change
Example: I wish I could dance.	I could take a dance class or practice dancing at home in front of a mirror.
1.	
2.	
3.	
4.	
5.	

Quiz Time!

Answer the following questions about Chapters 36–47.

1. Why does Crispin disobey Bear and leave him?

   _____

   _____

2. What does Crispin observe about Lady Furnival?

   _____

   _____

3. Why can't Crispin leave Great Wexly?

   _____

   _____

4. Why does Crispin fear that he and Bear have been trapped?

   _____

   _____

5. Why does the Widow Daventry give Crispin a job in the kitchen?

   _____

   _____

6. What does the Widow Daventry tell Crispin about Bear?

   _____

   _____

7. Why does John Ball want England to change?

   _____

   _____

8. Why do John Aycliffe and his soldiers take Bear away?

   _____

   _____

Baking Bread

Crispin escapes into the city and buys white bread from a vendor for a penny. He says, "It was light and sweet, and took little chewing to get down, which I found passing strange." Here is a recipe for the type of bread Crispin might have eaten. The recipe makes two loaves.

> **Warning:** Do NOT allow students to handle the knife or work near the oven. Be sure to ask parents if their children have any food allergies or dietary restrictions before allowing students to eat the bread.

Materials

- two large bowls
- measuring cups and spoons
- two loaf pans, approximately 9" x 5" x 3" (23 cm x 13 cm x 8 cm)
- a cooking thermometer
- cutting board (optional)
- rolling pin
- electric or hand-held mixer
- two dishtowels
- large, serrated knife
- oven mitts
- ruler or tape measure
- pastry brush
- small pan

Ingredients

- 6 to 7 cups (1.4 L to 1.7 L) all-purpose flour
- 3 tablespoons (45 mL) sugar
- 2 tablespoons (30 mL) shortening
- 2¼ cups (0.5 L) scalded milk cooled to about 120°F (48°C)
- 1 tablespoon (15 mL) salt
- 2 packages quick acting or active dry yeast
- jam, honey (optional)
- butter

Directions

1. Mix 3½ cups (0.8 L) of flour in a large bowl with sugar, salt, shortening, and yeast. Add warm milk and beat for about a minute. Stir in enough of the remaining flour, a cup (250 mL) or so at a time, until dough is easy to handle.

2. Turn the dough onto a lightly floured surface such as a countertop or cutting board. Knead, adding more flour as necessary to keep the dough from sticking, until it is smooth and elastic. This should take about 8 to 10 minutes.

3. Place the dough in a large buttered mixing bowl. Turn the dough over, greased side is up. Cover it with a clean dish towel and let it rise in a warm place for about one hour or until doubled.

4. Punch the dough down and divide it into two equal portions. With your hands or a rolling pin, flatten each half into two rectangles, each about 18 x 10 inches (46 cm x 26 cm). Starting at the 10-inch (26 cm) edge, roll the dough tightly. Pinch the long seam together. With the sides of your hands, press each end of the loaf. Fold the ends under the loaf. Place the loaves, seam side down, in the loaf pans. Melt some butter in a pan. Use a pastry brush to lightly coat the top of each loaf with butter. Loosely cover each loaf with a clean dish towel and let the dough rise until it has doubled, which takes about 35 to 50 minutes.

5. Preheat the oven to 425°F (220°C). Bake loaves on a low rack, so the tops of the pans are at the center of the oven. Bake for 25 to 30 minutes. The bread will sound hollow when lightly tapped.

6. Cool the bread slightly, then slice it with the serrated knife.

7. Serve the bread warm with butter, jam, and/or honey.

Famous Class Struggles

Bear is involved with a group of people who want to fight against the political system in medieval England in order to give all people equal rights. The lower class has always struggled for a better way of life — more food, decent housing, and higher wages. Crispin follows Bear to a building and hears a passionate voice declare, " '...that no man, or woman either, shall be enslaved, but stand free and equal to one another.' "

Work with two or three other students to do research about the class struggles listed below. Use the Internet, nonfiction books, and/or reference books to locate information about who was involved, when and where the struggle took place, why it occurred, and what the outcome was. Share your findings with the class.

1. **The Russian Revolution**

   Who? _____

   When? _____

   Where? _____

   Why? _____

   What outcome? _____

2. **The French Revolution**

   Who? _____

   When? _____

   Where? _____

   Why? _____

   What outcome? _____

3. **The American Revolution**

   Who? _____

   When? _____

   Where? _____

   Why? _____

   What outcome? _____

Sensory Details

As in the rest of *Crispin: The Cross of Lead*, Chapter 38 comes alive for the reader, thanks to Avi's use of sensory details — that is, details that appeal to one or more of the five senses.

Crispin describes the church in Great Wexly by saying, "Before me was a space of such immense size, height, depth, and breadth, that I never would have thought it could exist on mortal earth. Burning candles blossomed everywhere, enough to awe the stars. Through sweet and smoky air, great columns rose to dizzying heights, while enough multicolored light poured down through stained glass as to turn the hard stone floor into pools of liquid hues. From somewhere unseen a chorus of swelling chants rolled forth, filling this celestial space with sounds that made me think of the measured beating of angels' wings."

Use the chart below to write down any sensory details in the above description. One example is given.

Sense	Sensory Details
Sight	burning candles
Smell	
Sound	
Taste	
Touch	

Next write a description of your favorite place. Make your description come alive with as many sensory details as possible.

_____

_____

_____

_____

_____

_____

_____

Now that you are finished with your description, read it aloud to your class.

The Marketplace

Crispin has never seen a marketplace as exciting as the one in Great Wexly. He is astounded by the crowds of people, the food vendors, and the stalls full of goods for sale. Think about a local mall, farmers' market, grocery store, or another shopping area in your town. On the lines below, tell what Crispin might think if he visited this place.

Quiz Time!

Answer the following questions about Chapters 48–58.

1. According to the Widow Daventry, why might John Aycliffe torture Bear?

   _____

   _____

2. What does Crispin learn about the widow's family?

   _____

   _____

3. Why is Crispin's noble blood poison?

   _____

   _____

4. Why is Lady Furnival afraid that Lord Douglas will find out about Crispin?

   _____

   _____

5. Why does Crispin decide to try and free Bear?

   _____

   _____

6. How is the inside of the palace different from anything Crispin has ever seen?

   _____

   _____

7. Who does Crispin see in the picture in the palace?

   _____

   _____

8. At the end of the book, Bear says, "In the midst of death, there is life." What does this mean?

   _____

   _____

Candlemaking

In the fourteenth century, people could not switch on electric lights at night. They used candles to see in the dark. Here are instructions for making hand-dipped candles like those Crispin might have used.

> **Warning:** Use extreme caution when allowing students to make the candles. Do not allow students to handle the sharp knife.

Materials

- stove
- double broiler or large pot and large coffee tin
- pot holders
- 2-4 pounds (1-2 kg) of paraffin wax
- candle wicks, preferably the zinc core type
- crayons (one color with the paper removed)
- wax paper
- boiling water
- pot of cool water (optional)
- hangers
- a wooden spoon
- one or two essential oils
- sharp knife

> **Note:** The paraffin wax and candle wicks can usually be purchased at a hobby or craft store.

Directions

1. Melt the wax in a double broiler. If you do not have one, you can use a pot filled halfway with water and a large coffee tin. Heat the water until it is boiling. Once the water is boiling, turn down the heat. Cut up the paraffin and place it in the coffee tin. Use the pot holders to protect your hands as you place the coffee tin in the pot of hot water. Keep the water hot enough so that the wax stays melted, but do not make it so hot that the paraffin catches fire.

2. While the wax is melting, stir it with a wooden spoon. Make sure it is completely melted before trying to dip the wicks.

3. Break up the crayons and put them into the melted wax. Keep stirring until all of the crayons have melted and the color is even and smooth, with no streaks. The candle will be a shade or so lighter when dry. More crayons will produce a deeper, richer color.

4. Next add 10–20 drops of essential oil to the wax so it smells strongly of the fragrance. Now the wax is ready for dipping.

5. You will be making two candles at once, so start with a long piece of wick that is two times longer than your desired candle length, plus 3 inches (8 cm). Bend the wick in the middle and hold it at the bend. Using extreme caution, dip the wick into the wax and lift it back out. The wick will float on top of the paraffin until it has enough wax on it to weigh it down. When you first start, allow the wick to cool completely between dippings.

6. You can speed up the process after your candle has started to take shape by dipping the candles in a pot of cool water after dipping them in the wax.

7. Keep dipping the candles and allowing them to cool. When you have achieved a desirable size, hang the candles to dry until the wax has set but the candles are not too hard. Then roll them on the wax paper to smooth out the shape.

8. Finally, dip two more times to make sure your candles are smooth. Use a sharp knife to cut off the bottom of the candle so it is flat. Hang your candles to dry. Then cut the wick to separate the two candles. Trim each wick to the desired length.

The Gift of Reading

The Widow Daventry reads the words on Crispin's cross of lead. She tells him his mother must have been "some young, gentle lady who knew how to read and write." Reading was a valuable skill in the fourteenth century, just as it is today.

Give the gift of reading to a younger student. Bring your favorite children's books from home, or choose appropriate books from the school library. Spend an hour reading the books aloud to a younger student. When you are finished, fill out the form below.

My Name: _____

Name of Younger Student: _____

Titles of Books I Read: _____

_____

Description of My Experience: _____

_____

_____

_____

_____

_____

_____

_____

_____

The Renaissance World

Note to Teacher: Divide the class into groups of three or four students. Assign each group one of the topics listed below. Groups should not research the same topic.

Renaissance is a French word that means "new birth." The Renaissance was a period of time between the 1400s and 1600s. It is known for incredible inventions and accomplishments, some of which you will discover today.

Use the Internet, nonfiction books, and/or reference books to research your assigned Renaissance topic. Here is a list of possible topics:

- Art
- Literature
- Music
- Architecture

- Food
- Science
- Medicine
- Clothing

- Dance
- Astronomy
- Knights

Use the graphic organizer below to take notes. Use the notes to write a short report. Then present it to the class.

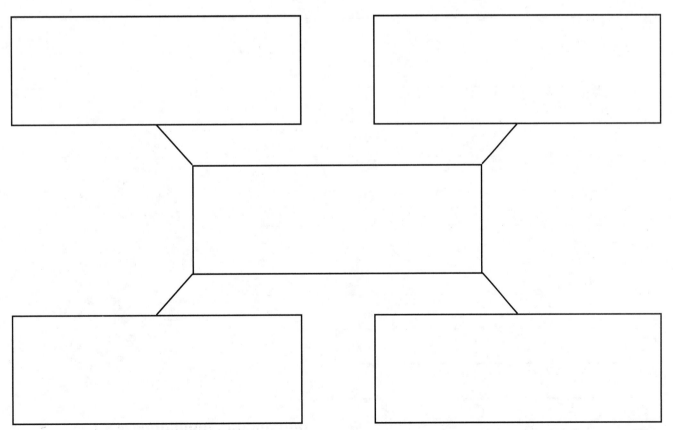

Courage

At the beginning of the novel, Crispin is a terrified boy, lacking in self-confidence. By the end of the novel, he shows tremendous courage when he rescues Bear and stands up to John Aycliffe and his soldiers. Crispin remarks, "As time passed in the darkness of my hiding place, the one thing I knew for sure was that as Bear had helped to free me, he had given me life. Therefore I resolved to help free him — even if it cost me that new life to do so."

Think of a time when you showed great courage. What was the situation? Who was involved? How did you feel before, during, and after this incident? What did you learn from it? Use the space below to write a descriptive story about your courageous action. Pay particular attention to sensory details.

_____

_____

_____

_____

_____

_____

_____

_____

_____

_____

_____

_____

_____

_____

_____

_____

_____

_____

Any Questions?

When you finished reading *Crispin: The Cross of Lead,* did you have questions that were left unanswered? Write some of your questions below.

1. _____

2. _____

3. _____

4. _____

5. _____

Work in groups or by yourself to predict possible answers for some or all of the questions you have asked above, as well as those written below. When you have finished, share your predictions with the class.

1. Do Crispin and Bear get captured again?
2. Does Lord Douglas find out about Crispin and claim the Furnival wealth?
3. Does Lady Furnival have Crispin killed?
4. Does Crispin ever return to Great Wexly?
5. Where do Bear and Crispin live?
6. How long do Bear and Crispin travel together?
7. Does Widow Daventry ever remarry?
8. Who takes over being steward after John Aycliffe's death?
9. What happens to the man with one eye?
10. Do rebels eventually change the class system in England?
11. Does Bear continue working as a spy?
12. Does Crispin ever return to Stromford?
13. What does Crispin become when he grows up?
14. Does Bear ever get married?
15. What do the soldiers think when they find the cross of lead?
16. Do other illegitimate children of Lord Furnival appear in Great Wexly?
17. Does Crispin abandon his religion?
18. Does Bear become more religious?
19. Does Crispin learn how to read and write? If so, who teaches him?
20. What happens to John Ball?
21. Does Crispin ever find someone who knew his mother at court?
22. Does Crispin ever marry?

Book Report Ideas

There are several ways to report on a book after you have read it. When you have finished *Crispin: The Cross of Lead,* choose a method of reporting from the list below, or come up with your own idea on how best to report on this book.

- **Make a Book Jacket**

  Design a book jacket for this book. On the front, draw a picture that you feel best captures this story. On the back, write a paragraph or two which summarizes the main points of the book.

- **Make a Time Line**

  On paper, create a time line to show the significant events in Crispin's life. You may illustrate your time line if you wish.

- **Design a Scrapbook**

  Use magazine pictures, photographs, and other illustrations to create a scrapbook that Crispin might keep to document his travels with Bear. He might choose to decorate his scrapbook with sketches of birds, trees, or the towns he sees. He might paste leaves and flowers into the scrapbook and include his beginning attempts at writing.

- **Make a Collage**

  Using old magazines and photographs, design a collage that illustrates all of Crispin's adventures in *Crispin: The Cross of Lead.*

- **Create a Time Capsule**

  What items might Crispin put in a time capsule to remember his travels with Bear? What container might he use as a time capsule?

- **Write a Biography**

  Do research to find out about the life of Avi. You may use the Internet (www.avi-writer.com) or magazines. Write a biography, showing how Avi's experiences might have influenced his writing of this novel.

- **Act Out a Play**

  With one or two other students, write a play featuring some of the characters in this novel. Then act out your play for the class.

- **Design a Diorama**

  Using a shoebox as a frame, create a diorama that illustrates an important scene in the novel. You may use all sorts of materials (paper, sand, clay, paint, fabric, etc.) to bring the scene to life.

- **Make Puppets**

  Using a variety of materials, design puppets to represent one or all of the characters in this novel. You may decide to work with other students to write and perform a puppet show.

Research Ideas

As you read *Crispin: The Cross of Lead,* you discovered people, geographic locations, and events about which you might wish to know more. To increase your understanding of the characters, places, and events in this novel, do research to gather additional information.

Work alone or in groups to find out about one or more of the items listed below. You may use nonfiction books, magazines, reference books, and/or the Internet. Afterwards, share your findings with the class.

- The Plague
- Medieval clothing
- Medieval food and drink
- Medieval manners
- Court jesters and entertainers
- Religion in fourteenth-century England
- King Edward the Third
- Medieval songs
- English cathedrals
- Wars between England and other countries
- Medieval houses and architecture
- Newbery Award
- Literacy in fourteenth-century England
- Medieval forms of punishment and torture
- Weapons of the fourteenth century
- Body language — specifically eye contact
- Medieval apothecaries
- Franciscan friars
- Medieval taverns
- Master and apprentice relationships
- Medieval flags
- Feast of John the Baptist
- Medieval stores and markets
- Flora and fauna of fourteenth-century England
- Medieval hunting techniques
- Movies depicting medieval times
- Medieval musical instruments
- Religious music of the fourteenth century
- Orphans during Medieval times
- Medieval spies
- Castles

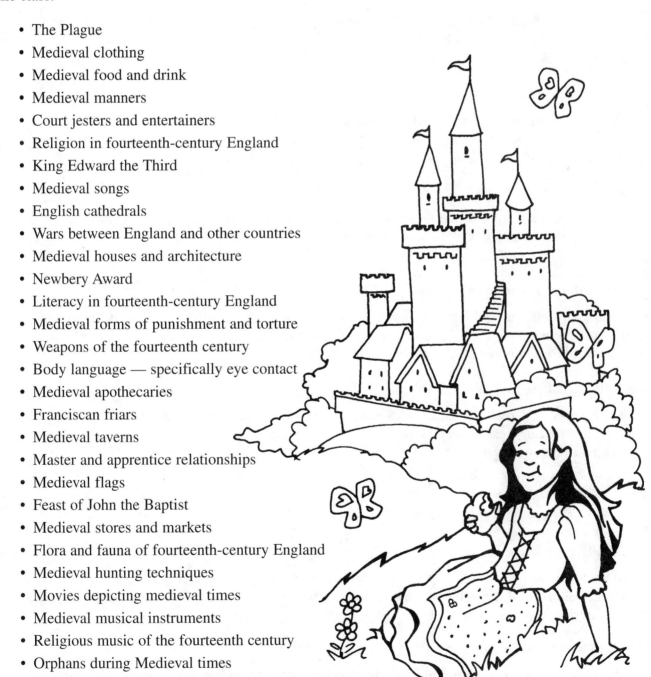

Field Trips and Class Visits

Now that your students have learned about the Renaissance world, they may enjoy taking one or more field trips related to those subjects. In addition, you may wish to invite guests to speak to your class. Choose an activity from the list below and locate the appropriate contact person in the phone book. Be sure to call at least three weeks in advance to give everyone plenty of time to prepare for the field trip or visit.

❑ **Renaissance Art**

Plan a trip to the local art museum to study the sculptures of Cellini, Donatello, Ghiberti, and Verrocchio. Marvel at paintings by Botticelli, Da Vinci, Michelangelo, Raphael, Titian, Bruegel, and Van Eyck.

❑ **Madrigal Music**

Does your community have a choir of madrigal singers? If so, invite them to come into your classroom for a performance, or take students to hear a concert. As an alternative, play madrigal music on tape in your classroom.

❑ **Astronomers**

Copernicus and Galileo of the Renaissance era were crucial to the study of astronomy. Invite a local astronomer to speak about their contributions to this science, or take a trip to the local planetarium to learn about their important discoveries.

❑ **Professional Entertainers**

Invite a professional children's entertainer to come to your classroom to teach students to juggle. Discuss the jesters of the fourteenth century in relation to contemporary entertainers. Ask your visitor to teach children Medieval songs and dances.

❑ **Living History**

The Society for Creative Anachronism is an international organization dedicated to recreating pre-17th century European history. You can find a local chapter by telephoning (800) 789-7486 or writing to the society at:

> Society for Creative Anachronism
> P.O. Box 360789
> Milpitas, CA 95036–0789

❑ **Renaissance Faire**

Many towns and cities hold an annual Renaissance Faire, dedicated to recreating the sights, sounds, smells, and food of the Renaissance era. Locate the fair that is closest to you and invite students on a field trip, or ask fair vendors to visit your classroom in costume.

❑ **The Play Is the Thing**

Shakespeare was the most prominent playwright of the Renaissance era. Take students to see a Shakespearean play, or watch videotapes of *A Midsummer Night's Dream, Much Ado About Nothing,* or *Romeo and Juliet.*

Renaissance Party

Why not invite your family or another class to your classroom to learn more about the Renaissance era? Students will enjoy planning, preparing for, and participating in their own party.

Party Checklist

Three weeks before the party…

❏ Decide when and where the party will occur.

❏ Discuss how you will incorporate the Renaissance theme into your party. Will you put Renaissance art on the walls? Will you play Renaissance music? Will you have a videotape showing one of Shakespeare's plays on the VCR? Will you dress in Renaissance costumes? Maybe you will make the classroom look like a castle.

❏ Talk about whom you want to invite. Perhaps you will want to invite the younger students to whom your students read (page 32). You may want to invite parents or other family members. Make and send invitations (page 40).

Two weeks before the party…

❏ Decide what food and drink you will make as a class. This book provides a recipe for bread (page 26). You may want to research foods eaten in the 14th, 15th, and 16th centuries and adjust your menu accordingly.

❏ Pass around a sign-up sheet. Each student should be encouraged to contribute something unique to the party. They might bring food, sign up to play the recorder, or juggle!

❏ Send home a note to students' parents to remind them of the party, and to let them know what students signed up to bring or do.

One week before the party…

❏ Send home a note reminding students of what they are to bring for the party.

❏ Buy and/or make decorations, including hand-dipped candles (page 31).

The day before the party…

❏ Bake bread (page 26).

The day of the party…

❏ Decorate the party space and set up a stage for student performances.

Enjoy!

Come to Our
Renaissance Party!

Date: _____

Time: _____

Place: _____

Hosts: _____

Activities: _____

Renaissance Clothing

People in Crispin's world did not dress like people today. Rich people sewed precious stones into their clothes — the more gems, the richer they were. Crispin is in awe of Lady Furnival's royal clothing when he sees her in Great Wexly. She even has a perfumed handkerchief to ward off the stench of the streets.

Study the pictures of the Renaissance man and woman. What do you notice about their style of dress? Color the pictures.

Rich and poor people dressed very differently during the Renaissance era. Use the Internet, nonfiction books, or reference books to learn how the clothing of wealthy people compared to the garments worn by peasants. List the major differences below. The first one is done for you.

Rich People

1. They wore expensive clothes with precious stones sewn into the fabric.

2. _____

3. _____

4. _____

5. _____

6. _____

Poor People

1. They wore clothes that were often dirty, torn, and threadbare.

2. _____

3. _____

4. _____

5. _____

Playing Marbles

Marbles have been found in archaeological digs dating back to the Ice Age on every continent. Renaissance painter Peiter Bruegel showed children playing marbles in his painting, "Children's Games" (1559). Shakespeare mentions playing marbles in his play *Twelfth Night*. Perhaps after they leave Great Wexly, Bear teaches Crispin to play marbles.

Materials

- one ½" (1.3 cm) marble for each student

- ¾" (1.9 cm) shooting marbles, one for each game

- chalk (optional)

Directions

1. This game is called "Ring Taw" or "Ringers." Divide the class into groups of six. For each group, draw a 10' (3 m) ring in the dirt. Then draw a 1' (30 cm) ring in the middle of the larger ring. As an alternative, you could use chalk to draw the rings on blacktop.

2. Determine the shooting order. Draw a line a little way away from the circles. Each student should kneel about 3' (91 cm) from the line and shoot a marble toward it to see who can get closest to the line. This is called "lagging." The student with the marble that is closest to the line shoots first in the game.

3. Each student places a ½" (1.3 cm) marble in the smaller ring. The first player starts outside the 10' (3 m) circle. The player points to the marble inside the smaller circle, which he/she will attempt to hit. Now, the player shoots the "taw" — a ¾" (1.9 cm) shooting marble, trying to knock this target marble out of the large ring while keeping the taw inside both rings. If the player succeeds, he/she shoots again from where the taw stopped.

4. If the player fails to knock the target marble out of the ring, or the taw goes outside the rings, the turn is over and the player to the left takes the next turn.

5. Play the game until all the marbles have been knocked out of the ring.

Objective Test and Essay

Matching: Match the description of each character with his or her name.

_____ 1. Crispin

_____ 2. Widow Daventry

_____ 3. Bear

_____ 4. Asta

_____ 5. John Aycliffe

_____ 6. Lady Furnival

_____ 7. John Ball

_____ 8. Goodwife Peregrine

_____ 9. Father Quinel

_____ 10. Great Wexly

a. declares Crispin a "wolf's head" and tries to have him murdered

b. could read and write, and had a son with Lord Furnival

c. helped Crispin bury his mother, then tried to help him escape

d. is afraid Lord Douglas will find out about Crispin and steal her power

e. helps Bear with his rebellion in order to give the people freedom

f. takes Bear and Crispin in, hides them, and feeds them

g. located behind stone walls, full of people, food, and other exiting things

h. loves Crispin like a son and teaches him how to survive

i. discovers amazing things about himself and his mother

j. gives Crispin a leather pouch for protection

True or False: Answer true or false in the blanks below.

1. _____ Crispin's mother did not know how to read or write.

2. _____ Crispin finds out that Bear is his father.

3. _____ Lady Furnival does not want Lord Douglas to find out about Crispin.

4. _____ Crispin is always confident and happy.

5. _____ Bear tries to help people earn freedom and fair pay.

Short Answer: On a separate sheet of paper, write a brief response to each question, using complete sentences.

1. Why does Crispin feel guilty of sin at the beginning of the book?

2. Why does Bear agree to help Crispin?

3. Why does John Aycliffe try to have Crispin killed?

4. Why were people mean to Crispin's mother, Asta, in Stromford Village?

5. How does Crispin show courage at the end of this book?

Essay: Respond to the following questions on a separate sheet of paper.

Bear asks Crispin, "Have you ever desired to be anything different from what you are?" Explain how Crispin changes during the course of this book. What is he like at the beginning? How does he grow? Who is responsible for helping him change?

Response

On a separate sheet of paper, explain and respond to the following quotations as selected by your teacher.

Chapter 2:   *Two men were standing in a clearing. One was John Aycliffe. In one hand he held a fluttering torch. As always, a sword was at his side.*

Chapter 4:   *The cottage, being of small, mean construction, could not withstand their assault. Within moments it was little more than a heap of thatch, wattle, and clay.*

Chapter 11:   *It was Father Quinel. He lay very still. 'Father?' I called softly. He did not answer.*

Chapter 13:   *The truth was — and how great my shame — I no longer wished to live; which was, I knew, a sin.*

Chapter 21:   *'You'll practice more. You'll add more balls as you go. Music, too.'*

Chapter 25:   *'Think what you might become if you were cleansed of thirteen years of dirt, neglect, and servitude.'*

Chapter 29:   *'Crispin, I'm part of a . . . brotherhood. It's to make things better. To bring some change.'*

Chapter 34:   *We fairly well danced our way up to the gate and through the town walls with not so much as an unkind look from anyone.*

Chapter 37:   *As I went about, the hurly-burly world of countless people, buildings and wares, struck me with even greater force.*

Chapter 41:   *'But if we are to talk of Furnival's heirs, in my travels I've discovered something of great importance.'*

Chapter 44:   *'You've been protecting me,' I said. 'Maybe I should be protecting you.'*

Chapter 45:   *'...that no man, or woman either, shall be enslaved, but stand free and equal to one another.'*

Chapter 49:   *'Crispin, I can not be certain, but if the rumor of the time — thirteen years ago — was true, I believe I know who your mother was.'*

Chapter 56:   *'It reads, 'Crispin — son of Furnival.' '*

Chapter 58:   *And my name — I knew with all my heart — was Crispin.*

Conversations

Work in groups according to the numbers in parentheses to write or act out the conversations that might have occurred in *Crispin: The Cross of Lead*.

- Lord Furnival tells Asta she must live in the village of Stromford without him. (2 people)

- John Aycliffe and Lord Furnival talk about what do to with Asta and her son. (2 people)

- Father Quinel, Goodwife Peregrine, and Asta talk about why Crispin cannot know the truth about his father. (3 people)

- Father Quinel tells Crispin the truth about his parents. (2 people)

- Bear meets John Aycliffe and tries to keep him from finding out about Crispin. (2 people)

- Bear and Crispin return to Stromford and talk to Goodwife Peregrine about Great Wexly. (3 people)

- Bear and the Widow Daventry talk about the danger that Crispin faces. (2 people)

- Bear and John Ball talk to peasants about how they deserve freedom. (4 people)

- Crispin talks to the Widow Daventry about his feelings regarding religion. (2 people)

- John Aycliffe confronts Father Quinel about helping Crispin before he murders the priest. (2 people)

- Lady Furnival and Crispin argue with each other. (2 people)

- Lady Furnival, John Aycliffe, and the steward talk about what to do about Crispin. (3 people)

- Lord Douglas and Bear discuss Crispin, who is Lord Furnival's son. (3 people)

- Bear and John Ball talk to Lady Furnival about peasants' rights. (3 people)

- Crispin prays to St. Giles after he leaves Great Wexly, and pretends to have a conversation with the saint. (2 people)

- Lady Furnival demands that the Widow Daventry tell her where Crispin has gone. (2 people)

- The Widow Daventry tells Crispin about her first husband. (2 people)

Bibliography of Related Reading

━━━━━━━━━━━━━━━━━━━━━━━━━━━ **Fiction** ━━━━━━━━━━━━━━━━━━━━━━━━━━━

Avi. *Midnight Magic.* (Scholastic, 1999)

Cooper, Susan. *King of Shadows.* (Aladdin, 2001)

Cushman, Karen. *Catherine Called Birdy.* (HarperTrophy, 2002)

Cushman, Karen. *Matilda Bone.* (Yearling, 2002)

De Angeli, Marguerite. *The Door in the Wall.* (Yearling, 1990)

Garinger, Alan. *Torch in the Darkness: The Tale of a Boy Artist in the Renaissance.* (Guild Press of Indiana, 2000)

Pressler, Mirjam. *Shylock's Daughter.* (Phyllis Fogleman Books, 2001)

━━━━━━━━━━━━━━━━━━━━━━━━━━━ **Nonfiction** ━━━━━━━━━━━━━━━━━━━━━━━━━━━

Bingham, Jane. *Medieval World.* (Usborne Pub, Ltd., 1999)

Canta, Lillo. *The Renaissance: The Invention of Perspective.* (Chelsea House, 1995)

Cole, Alison. *Eyewitness: Renaissance.* (DK Publishing, 2000)

Dale-Weir, Catherine. *Coat of Arms.* (Grosset & Dunlap, 2000)

Morley, Jacqueline. *A Renaissance Town.* (Peter Bedrick Books, 2001)

Spence, David. *Michelangelo and the Renaissance.* (Barrons' Education Series, 1997)

Stanley, Diane and Vennema, Peter. *Good Queen Bess: The Story of Elizabeth I of England.* (HarperCollins, 2001)

Stanley, Diane. *Michelangelo.* (HarperCollins, 2000)

Tiernay, Tom. *Italian Renaissance Costumes Paper Dolls.* (Dover, 1998)

Tiernay, Tom. *Renaissance Fashions.* (Dover, 2000)

Answer Key

Page 10

1. Asta says Crispin's father died in the Great Mortality (the Plague).

2. Crispin witnesses John Aycliffe and a stranger talking and exchanging a parchment.

3. Men burn the house in which Crispin grew up.

4. Crispin is labeled "a wolf's head" because John Aycliffe accuses him of stealing.

5. The people in the village do not believe Crispin stole from the manner. The fact is exposed when Crispin overhears two men talking.

6. The priest tells Crispin his mother could read and write, and that she named him Crispin.

7. Goodwife Peregrine gives Crispin a leather pouch, as well as porridge and a sack of food.

8. Crispin is led into a trap.

Page 15

1. Crispin finds three seeds in the pouch and throws them away.

2. Crispin sees a dead man swinging from a gallows, and the sight makes him want to stay alive.

3. Bear is upset about the class inequalities; he doesn't care for England's government.

4. Having unlawfully left his master, Crispin becomes servant to the first free man who finds him.

5. Reading could keep a person alive in the fourteenth century, since it elevated one to the level of a priest.

6. Crispin learns that Lord Furnival is arrogant and cruel, with a fondness for women.

7. Bear says that Crispin will find freedom if he loses his sorrows.

8. If Crispin were to live by questions, they would be about his parents, and about his own fate.

Page 20

1. Bear wants Crispin to realize he can be different than who he is.

2. Crispin realizes Bear is rough, but kind.

3. Bear teaches Crispin to play the recorder in order to accompany him as he juggles and sings.

4. The village of Lodgecot reminds Crispin of Stromford because people are hard at work, and there are sheep and cattle.

5. Crispin observes the angry one-eyed man staring at him.

6. Bear teaches Crispin that a man's soul may be observed behind his eyes; therefore, it's important to make eye contact.

7. Crispin decides to trust Bear. They begin to have genuine affection for each other.

8. Crispin and Bear play and sing through the gates of Great Wexly.

Page 22

Tracking Observations

1. There's a stranger at the door.

2. Dawn is approaching.

3. There will be six more weeks of winter.

4. Spring is here.

5. This indicates autumn.

6. Colder weather is coming.

7. It is summer.

8. There is a hawk or other predator overhead.

9. Winter is coming.

10. It is winter.

Page 23

Renaissance Personalities

1. Donatello; Italian sculptor, first to work with bronze.

2. Marco Polo; Explorer; gave Europeans some of the earliest information on China.

3. Michelangelo Buonarroti; Painter and sculptor; painted the Sistine Chapel.

4. Christopher Columbus; Explorer; discovered the coast of South America, the West Indies, and Central America.

5. Galileo Galilei; Scientist; one of the chief founders of modern science, he invented the telescope.

6. Catherine De Medici; Politician and patron of the arts; her money and interest helped the arts to flourish.

7. William Shakespeare; Playwright and poet; wrote some of the greatest plays and sonnets of all time.

8. Rene Descartes; Philosopher, scientist, and mathematician; considered the father of modern philosophy.

9. Isabella d'Este; Ruler of Mantua; she was a patron of the arts and invited artists into her home.

10. Elizabeth I – Queen of England; encouraged architecture, the first theater, poetry, music. She avoided war with Roman Catholic nations.

Answer Key *(cont.)*

Page 25

1. Crispin disobeys Bear and leaves because he is curious about the town and wants to claim his liberties.

2. Crispin observes Lady Furnival's rich clothing. She presses a cloth to her nose to ward off the stench.

3. Crispin can't leave Great Wexly because the gates are shut at night.

4. Crispin sees the one-eyed man in the tavern and has the sensation that danger is near.

5. The Widow Daventry gives Crispin a job in the kitchen because she is trying to hide his identity from those who are looking for him.

6. The Widow Daventry tells Crispin that she would prefer him to juggle and make music instead of helping with the rebellion.

7. John Ball wants England to change because he says all people deserve their freedom.

8. John Aycliffe and the soldiers take Bear away because they're trying to find Crispin.

Page 30

1. John Aycliffe might torture Bear to find out where Crispin is hiding.

2. Crispin learns that the Widow Daventry had two husbands and seven children, all dead.

3. Crispin's noble blood is poison because Lady Furnival sees him as the enemy.

4. Lady Furnival is afraid Lord Douglas will find out about Crispin and make a claim to the Furnival wealth.

5. Crispin decides to try and free Bear because Bear had helped to free him and give him life.

6. The inside of the palace is richly decorated, with the remains of a huge feast.

7. Crispin sees his father in the picture.

8. Bear means that although John Aycliffe (and/or Asta) was killed, he and Crispin have gained their freedom.

Page 43

Matching

1. i	6. d	
2. f	7. e	
3. h	8. j	
4. b	9. c	
5. a	10. g	

True or False

1. False
2. False
3. True
4. False
5. True

Short Answer

1. Crispin feels guilty of sin because no one in his village talks to him. After his house is burned down, he is convinced that God is punishing him.

2. Bear agrees to help Crispin because he likes the boy, and because he wants to protect Lord Furnival's son.

3. John Aycliffe is afraid his own position will be in danger if Lord Douglas realizes Crispin is his grandson. Lord Douglas could seize Lord Furnival's wealth.

4. People were mean to Asta because she had a child out of wedlock. Also, she could read and write, and she was beautiful, which may have separated her from the others.

5. Crispin shows courage by standing up to John Aycliffe and rescuing Bear.

Essay

Answers will vary. Accept reasonable and well-supported answers.

Page 44

Grade students on their comprehension of the story as evidenced by the lengths of answers and depths of responses.

Page 45

Grade students on comprehension of the story, knowledge of the characters, and creativity.